I0100287

This Book Belongs To:

_____

HOPE
ARISE

The Unexpected Guest

by April Foster

Illustrated by Avery Leighton

Integrity Publishing LLC
www.bookswithintegrity.com

Copyright © 2024 by April Foster

Illustrations copyright © 2024 by Avery Leighton

All rights reserved. This book or parts thereof may not be reproduced in any form, stored in any retrieval system, or transmitted in any form by any means—electronic, mechanical, photocopy, recording, or otherwise—without prior written permission of the author or publisher, except as provided by United States of America copyright law. For permission requests, contact the author or write to the publisher, at "Attention: Permissions," at the web address below.

Published in Augusta, Georgia, by Integrity Publishing LLC. www.bookswithintegrity.com

Unless otherwise noted, Scripture quotations are taken from the Holy Bible, New International Version®, NIV®,Copyright © 1973, 1978, 1984, 2011 by Biblica, Inc.® Used by permission. All rights reserved worldwide.

Scripture quotations marked (NLT) are taken from the Holy Bible, New Living Translation, Copyright © 1996, 2004, 2007 by Tyndale House Foundation. Used by permission of Tyndale House Publishers, Inc., Carol Stream, Illinois 60188. All rights reserved.

For more information on the author, visit www.lovecoloredtheway.com

Library of Congress Control Number: 2024924545

ISBN: 978-1-953822-08-6

Publisher's Cataloging-in-Publication Data

Names: Foster, April. | Leighton, Avery.

Title: The Unexpected Guest / by April Foster : illustrated by Avery Leighton.

Description: Augusta: Integrity Publishing 2024.

Summary: "Author April Foster delights readers with a story of hope in the waiting, told through the supernatural transformation of a caterpillar into a butterfly."—Provided by publisher.

Identifiers: LCCN 2024924545 | ISBN 978-1-953822-08-6 (hardback)

Subjects: CYAC: 1. Hope. 2. Caterpillars. 3. Butterflies. | BISAC: JUVENILE NONFICTION / Religious / Christian/Science & Nature. | JUVENILE NONFICTION / Animals / Butterflies, Moths & Caterpillars. | JUVENILE NONFICTION / Religious / Christian / Inspirational.

Cover Design by Sara McGee and Holly Murray

Interior Format by Holly Murray

Editing by Holly Murray

Photography by Wendi Rae Leighton For more information, visit www.facebook.com/profile.php?id=61550715126731

Printed in the United States of America

24 25 26 27 28 10 9 8 7 6 5 4 3 2 1

To my beloved daughter Emery,

This story began with a beautiful bouquet of flowers you gifted me on my birthday. Hidden within that bouquet was a tiny surprise-a caterpillar egg-which inspired a tale of hope and wonder. As the little caterpillar devoured the flowers, it reminded me of how you devoured books with the same eagerness and joy. Your love of books inspired me to write one of my own.

I love you to the moon and back!

Love,
Mom

A birthday gift arrived at my door. It was a vase full of flowers in the most amazing colors. I smelled the sweet blossoms, but didn't notice a tiny object hidden among the stems.

Three days later, something strange happened—some flowers had vanished!

Looking closely, I found a glorious green, yellow, black, and white squiggly little caterpillar. He appeared quite at home in my bouquet, munching away.

I took lots of pictures and videos of my hungry caterpillar as he ate the yummy dill flowers, one after another.

Crunch, munch, nibble, gulp!

As the dill dwindled, I was worried he would soon be out of food! Where could I find more dill flowers?

The florist who delivered the flowers said she would come pick up my hungry little caterpillar. I told her I wanted to keep him! He just needed more food to eat—he was very hungry!

we are so sorry we will take the caterpillar back

My caterpillar was growing. Chomp, chomp, chomp!
He devoured one flower after another.

One week later, the caterpillar stopped eating
and rested all day. He formed a chrysalis.

In nine to eighteen days, something amazing would happen—the caterpillar would emerge from its chrysalis. With each passing day, my excitement grew.

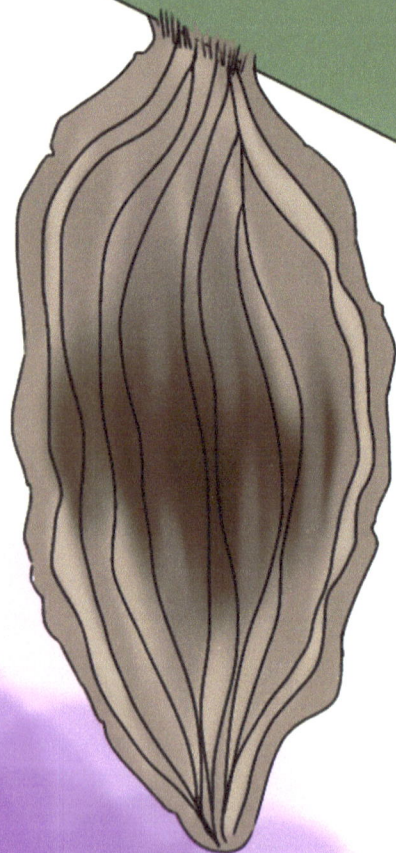

REC

HATCH DAY!

12	13	14
19	20	21
26		

I set up a security camera to watch from my phone when I wasn't home. What would he look like? How much longer would I need to wait?

More weeks flew by. Was my caterpillar dead? Had I done something wrong? It was taking forever!

Maybe if I held my breath and counted . . .

One . . .

Two . . .

Three!

Weeks turned to months, and winter arrived. I felt sad. I painted a picture and placed it under the chrysalis. It reminded me to have hope that I would see my little friend again.

HOPE ARISE

I no longer watched the chrysalis every day. I put it on the windowsill in the bathroom, almost forgotten. With a tiny bit of hope, I'd spray a little water on it to keep it from drying out, wondering if something in there was still alive.

Spring finally arrived, and with it, warmer days. New plants sent up bright green shoots, reaching for the sun. I placed the chrysalis outside, hoping the warmth might help bring it to life.

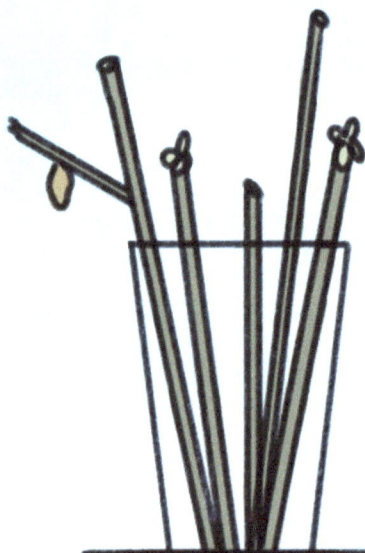

The next day, a huge storm blew in with fierce winds.
The trees shook, and the windows rattled.
I pulled the chrysalis inside and placed it on a glass table under a plant.

A week later, I noticed a strange, wax-like substance had dripped onto the table. I glanced at the chrysalis. It was empty!

Excitedly, I looked around for a butterfly, expecting to see its delicate, colorful wings fluttering nearby. But he wasn't there! I searched and searched, but there was no butterfly in sight. Where could he be?

My eyes shifted to movement near the floor. And there—magnificent and fully spread out—was a stunning Black Swallowtail butterfly. I couldn't believe what I was seeing!

I crouched down beside the beautiful creature. I didn't touch him; his wings were still damp and delicate.

I gazed in wonder
as he flapped and
fluttered his wings.
His strength and
confidence grew as
he practiced flying.

I placed a net over the butterfly and observed my colorfully spotted friend. What once was just a hope had come to life nine months later!

I loved my butterfly and wanted to keep him.
But butterflies weren't designed to be held
captive. They were created to fly freely.

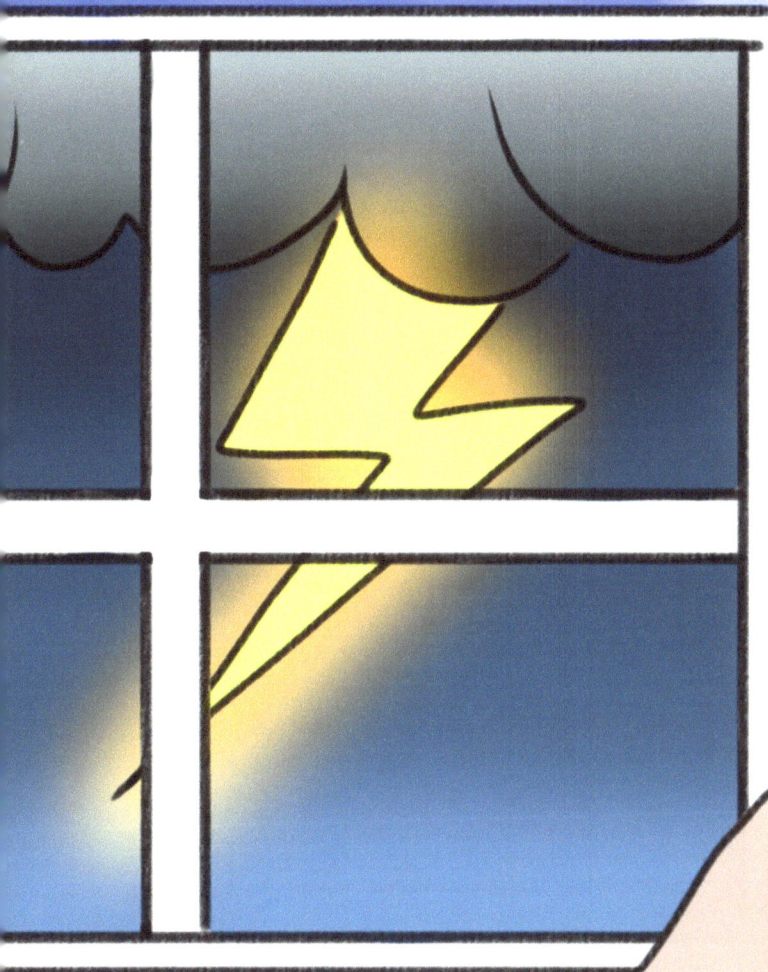

I peered out of my window. The weather was cold, cloudy, and rainy. Tomorrow's forecast would be sunny and warm.

SUNNY

I arose the next morning, placed the cage on the green grass, and gently opened the top. The butterfly paused before flying out as if to say, "Thank you—I've enjoyed the journey, but now it's time for me to soar."

I watched the butterfly flutter with energy and strength. He twirled joyfully before landing on the tallest tree!

Most butterflies live 14 days. That seems so short, but to the butterfly, it's a lifetime.

Lessons from the Black Swallowtail:

Don't lose hope—even when things don't seem to progress as quickly as you planned. Sometimes, we go through transformations that take longer than we expected (Psalms 37:5).

Jesus died so that everyone who believes in Him would have eternal life (John 3:16). But He didn't stay dead. Three days later, He rose and came out of an empty tomb. When you see an empty chrysalis hanging on a stalk or branch, let it remind you that Jesus is alive!

Hope believes something is possible. Faith believes it will happen, even before you see it with your eyes. God is pleased when we have faith to believe what He says in His Word (Hebrews 11:6).

More Lessons from the Black Swallowtail:

God's promises belong to us forever and fill us with hope while we remain on the earth. Like the butterfly, we, too, wait with hope for the day when God will give us our full rights as His adopted children, including the new bodies He has promised us (Romans 8:18-25).

There will come a day when we, too, will experience that final transformation and spend forever with Jesus in Heaven (John 5:24).

In the time of waiting, remember to live your life to the fullest, doing all God has put in you to do. Even when growing feels long and hard, trust that God is working in and through you, preparing you for something beautiful and new (Jeremiah 29:11).

Discussion Questions:

- What are the four parts of the lifecycle of the butterfly?

- If you found a caterpillar in a bunch of flowers, what would you do?

- Where do you think the butterfly went after he flew to the top of the tree?

- Have you ever expected something to happen quickly and then it took longer than you thought it would? What was it? Was it worth the wait?

Challenge:

- Watch a video of a caterpillar transforming into a chrysalis.

"Now faith is confidence in what we hope for and assurance about what we do not see."

Hebrews 11:1, NIV

Inspiration for the Story

Waiting has never been my strong suit—but who finds waiting easy? Does the wait make the reward sweeter? Absolutely. Often, we don't understand the process, but in the end, it's worth it.

Avery, the illustrator, saw a story I hadn't realized was there. She was at my house when the caterpillar transformed into a chrysalis. Later, as I shared a journal entry I wrote after releasing the butterfly, Avery asked, "Can I draw the cover for your book?" Laughing, I responded, "What book?"

I created a video showcasing the photos and footage I had captured over nine months. After pitching the idea to Holly Murray at Integrity Publishing, this book was born!

If you'd like to see the video featuring the real caterpillar, chrysalis, and butterfly, visit lovecoloredtheway.com or scan the QR code below.

About the Author:

April Foster grew up in the charming town of Hammond, Louisiana, and now travels the country with her husband of 29 years, exploring new places and enjoying adventure at every turn. From scuba diving in the deep blue sea to hiking towering mountains or riding wild roller coasters, April embraces every thrill. A lifelong lover of storytelling, she cherished reading to her now-adult children, as she shared stories that sparked imagination and joy. Her debut children's book captures the same adventurous spirit she holds dear, that every day is a new chance to discover something amazing. Her stories inspire young readers to dream big and explore the wonders of the world God created.

About the Illustrator:

Avery Leighton is a 15-year-old with a passion for visual storytelling. Since the age of six, she has developed a strong foundation in technique and composition. As a newcomer to the children's book industry, Avery combines creativity and precision to bring a fresh, detail-oriented perspective to her work. Her ten years in Classical Conversations enriched her homeschool education, fostering an appreciation for narrative structure that enhances her illustrations. When not drawing, Avery enjoys playing volleyball, spending time with her family and three sisters, hanging out with friends, and indulging in Cane's chicken. She is excited to expand her artistic journey and inspire young readers with her unique vision.

Acknowledgements:

This children's book is the result of incredible teamwork and dedication. My deepest gratitude goes to my editor, Holly Murray, for her insightful guidance, my illustrator, Avery Leighton, for bringing the story to life with stunning artwork, and my cover designers, Sara McGee and Holly Murray, for creating a beautiful and inviting cover. Your talents and commitment have made this dream a reality.

To my husband, John, thank you for your steadfast love and support in pursuing my dreams.

Above all, I give glory to Jesus, my Lord and Savior, for working through me and making this journey possible.

A Word from the Author:

If you enjoyed *The Unexpected Guest*, please take a moment to leave a heartfelt review. Your kind feedback is appreciated and helps others discover this delightful, true story. Thank you!

Design a Butterfly:

www.ingramcontent.com/pod-product-compliance
Lightning Source LLC
Chambersburg PA
CBHW041539260326
41914CB00015B/1503